Gonzo's Little Book of Motivation

David A. Kelly

Linda –
Thank you for all you do
to serve !   Dave Kelly
3/17/07

Bloomington, IN   authorHOUSE®   Milton Keynes, UK

AuthorHouse™
1663 Liberty Drive, Suite 200
Bloomington, IN 47403
www.authorhouse.com
Phone: 1-800-839-8640

AuthorHouse™ UK Ltd.
500 Avebury Boulevard
Central Milton Keynes, MK9 2BE
www.authorhouse.co.uk
Phone: 08001974150

First published by AuthorHouse 10/31/2006

ISBN: 1-4259-5767-6 (sc)

*Printed in the United States of America
Bloomington, Indiana*

This book is printed on acid-free paper.

Acknowledgements

This book is possible because over the years so many people have believed in me and supported me.

I thank my family for shaping me into the man I am today and giving me so much material for my speeches and articles; Stan and Jim, the first people who really believed in me; Miss Due, who encouraged me to write; Mike, who recognized the leader that I could become; the University of Wisconsin-Oshkosh for helping me to fulfill my dream of a college education; and all of the friends who ever encouraged me: Barry, Beth, Carol, Ann, Dave, Mark, Lanton, Lori, Brian, Katherine, Kevin, Frank, Bob, Bill, Greg, Shawn, Carolyn, David, Larry, George, Shannon, Bob, Abby, Mike, Stan, and Diane.

I owe an incredible debt of gratitude to two organizations that have shaped my career and presented me with many fantastic opportunities. The first is the Kiwanis International Family which provided me with my pivotal moment when I was 16. I have been incredibly blessed by this organization and especially by the Key Leader program, and the Wisconsin-Upper Michigan and Georgia Districts of Key Club, Circle K, and Kiwanis. I am very thankful for the encouragement and blessing of my Georgia Circle K Governors: Julie, Jennifer, Carol, Rebecca, Devin, John, Patsy, Katie, and Blaire.

The second is the Association for the Promotion of Campus Activities (APCA). I am so thankful for Eric, Dave, Tasha, and Jessica. I am also grateful for my fellow

APCA speakers and friends who have been so encouraging to me: Victor, Elizabeth, Patrick, Deanna, Troy, Peter, Kevin, Jonathon, Randy, James, Brian, Barbara, and Del. Thanks also to all of the students and advisors who have supported my programs and presentations.

I extend my deepest appreciation to the following individuals for opening various doors for me: Phil, Walter, Jem, Lacey, Jim, Lovell, Justina, Dhanfu, Dr. Shirley, Dianna, Dr. Tim, Christie, Johnnie, and everyone else who has believed in me enough to hire me to speak at their campus, company, church, or organization.

None of this would be possible without those who support and love me and put up with my travel schedule and late night writing sessions: my daughters Amanda and Katie, and my wife Dia, who is my soul-mate, confidant, business partner, and editor. It is so wonderful to spend each day with my best friend in the world.

Finally, I would not be here without the love and blessing of my Father in Heaven and my Lord and Savior, Jesus Christ. I am thankful for the talents and abilities He has placed within me.

Dave "Gonzo" Kelly

Welcome!

This is my first book and I am very excited that you are reading it.

I believe that each of us has the innate ability and talent to accomplish great things. Unfortunately, too often we give in to our self-doubts or the well-meaning "advice" of people who are close to us. Allowing this approach to govern our thinking puts us in the position of failing to pursue the things we really want out of life. I allowed this to happen for the first 20 years of my life after college and I was miserable. Now I am pursuing my passions and finding the life that God always intended for me.

I encourage you to use this book as a tool for your personal success. Review it often. Pick a quote and post it in a place that is visible to you daily and then rotate it out daily or weekly. Find quotes or thoughts that are especially meaningful to you and memorize them so they become a part of who you are.

Finally, feel free to share your favorite quotes with me (including those not in this book) by emailing me at davekelly@gonzospeaks.com.

Here's to your success!

Dave "Gonzo" Kelly

Gonzo's Little Book of Motivation

"Whatever you can do,
or dream you can,
begin it.

Boldness has genius,
power, and magic in it."

Johann Wolfgang von Goethe
(1749-1832)

Anything you desire to do, begin it.

Don't wait for all conditions to be "perfect".

Start.

Dreams are too important not to pursue them.

*"A career is not
a place you go
to collect a pay check
and hide out for 40 years."*

Dave Kelly

A career is doing the one thing in life that you would do for free, yet you have found a way to get paid for what you love.

"You miss 100% of the shots you don't take."

Wayne Gretzky
Hockey Hall of Famer

You will never accomplish anything unless you try.

"The only person who can stop you from reaching your goals is you."

Jackie Joyner-Kersee
Athlete

Get out of your own way.

Believe you can achieve.

Make your goals happen.

"Speak from the heart and people will listen."

Dave Kelly

You have incredible information,
stories, and ideas to share.

Don't just tell a person
(or an audience)
what they want to hear.

Speaking from the heart gives
you genuine credibility.

*"Goal attainment
is a never-ending journey
with infinite destinations
and victories too numerous
to count."*

Dave Kelly

Set and attain goals every day,
until you draw your final breath.

Then all of your days will
be filled with energy and
excitement.

"Ask and ye shall receive,
seek and ye shall find,
knock and it will be opened
unto you.

For he who asks receives,
he who seeks finds,
and to him who knocks,
the door will be opened."

Luke 11:9-10

The realization of your dreams is going to require some effort on your part.

Do what you need to do and let God do what He's going to do.

"Just because
you have a title
does not mean
you are leader.

Lead by example
and others will follow."

Dave Kelly

Go and do.

That's leadership.

Then invite others to join you and stick with the example you have set.

"If you want to know how to get somewhere, ask the person who is already there."

Dr. Allen Hunt
Pastor, Author and Radio Personality

The best way to speed up the process of accomplishing your goals in life – to do what you *really* want to do – is to find someone who is already doing it and learn from them.

*"Make mistakes
when the stakes
are not too high."*

Dave Kelly

Don't be afraid of trying new things in school, organizations, church, even work.

The learning experiences you have with little things will prepare you to deal with the big things in life.

"There will be
only one of you
for all time.

Fearlessly,
be yourself."

Anonymous

You can be the best
in the world at something—
being you.

Choose to be a
"world champion" you.

"If opportunity doesn't knock, build a door."

Milton Berle
(1908-2002)

Opportunity is right before you—but you have to be able to get to it.

Don't wait for things to come to you.

Go make them happen.

*"How do you eat
an elephant?*

One bite at a time."

Ancient Proverb

Don't allow yourself to be overwhelmed by the tasks before you.

Pick one and complete it.

Then do it again.

Repeat until finished.

Don't allow the "elephant" to be a de-motivator to the point that you do not accomplish anything at all.

"Before you hit
the ground running,
hit your knees praying."

Dave Kelly

The momentum of life
can overwhelm you
if you do not first ask God
to go before you.

*"This is the day
which the
Lord has made.*

*Let us rejoice
and be glad in it."*

Psalm 118:24

Every day is a gift
to be enjoyed.

Make each day a success
through an attitude of joy.

"If you think
you can do a thing,
or think you can't do a thing,
you're right."

Henry Ford
(1863-1947)

Barriers, obstacles, and limitations are only in your mind.

If you choose not to accept them, then they are not real.

You can push past them by *seeing* yourself pushing past them.

"The pessimist looks at opportunities and sees difficulties; the optimist sees difficulties and sees new opportunities."

Anonymous

Opportunities are
all around us.

Seek them out and
make the most of them.

*"Think outside
of the box
before you are put in one."*

Dave Kelly

Life is about stepping out and creating awesome new things—books, movies, organizations, etc.

Only by "thinking outside of the box" can you create an advance in human history.

"*Perfection
is not attainable.*

*But if we
chase perfection,
we can catch excellence.*"

Vince Lombardi
(1913-1970)

Are you willing to do
whatever it takes
to do what you do
to perfection?

Lombardi was.

And in seven years, he won
five world championships.

Be the world champion of
your life.

Excellence will ensue.

"Accepting barriers and obstacles is unacceptable."

Dave Kelly

Push past the barriers and obstacles in your way.

Do not accept them.

Rather, convince yourself of your possibilities.

"Being defeated
is often a temporary condition.

Giving up is what makes
it permanent."

Marilyn vos Savant
National Columnist and Author

Be your own "comeback"
superstar and grab victory out of
the jaws of defeat.

If you never quit,
then you will never fail.

"Obstacles are those frightful things you see when you take your eyes off your goal."

Henry Ford
(1863-1947)

Keep your eyes on your goals and dreams.

Don't ever let obstacles, limitations, or barriers into even your peripheral vision—let alone your plain sight.

*"Give me a chance and
I will change the world."*

Dave Kelly

There is one great gift
you can give anyone:
opportunity.

*"It's kind of fun
to do the impossible."*

Walt Disney
(1901-1966)

What impossible things do you imagine or visualize?

Make them happen.

You <u>could</u> be the world's next creative genius.

"'For I know the plans
I have for you,'
declares the Lord.

'Plans to prosper you and
not to harm you,
plans to give you
hope and a future.

Then you will
call upon me and
come and pray to me,
and I will listen to you.'"

Jeremiah 29:11-12

If the Creator of the Universe has a vested interest in your happiness and prosperity, then shouldn't you as well?

*"Have a little laugh
and look around for happiness
instead of sadness."*

Red Skelton
(1913-1997)

Happiness is both a joy and a choice.

Given the choice between happiness and misery,
I choose happiness.

"Do not fear conflict:
embrace it,
confront it,
deal with it.

Then turn it
into a victory
for everyone involved."

Dave Kelly

Treat conflicts as opportunities
and teachable moments.

Seek a "win-win" solution
and you will usually achieve
the best result.

"Only passions,
great passions,
can elevate the soul
to great things."

Denis Diderot
(1713-1784)

Pursue your passions
with passion.

You will be blessed by God
with answers to your prayers.

And He will lead your soul
to incredible accomplishments
that will last an eternity.

"If you want to make an apple pie from scratch, you must first create the universe."

Dr. Carl Sagan
(1934-1996)

Don't expect the "playing field" for your hopes and dreams to already exist.

It might not.

Create your own opportunities and then fulfill them.

"Organize to prioritize.

Success doesn't happen in a mess."

Dave Kelly

By being organized and
prioritizing your work,
you will be able to accomplish
tasks systematically.

I find it impossible to concentrate
on the task at hand if all the
others are staring me
in the face.

"If you wait
for the perfect moment
when all is safe
and assured,
it may never arrive.

Mountains
will not be climbed,
races won,
or lasting happiness achieved."

Maurice Chevalier
(1888-1972)

There are no perfect moments.

Whatever you want to do or
achieve, begin your pursuit.

You will give your "want"
energy and excitement that will
lead to the accomplishment of
your goals and dreams.

"*Put on
the best show
for the people
who show up.*"

Dave Kelly

No matter how many people attend an event or presentation that you are involved with, always give the audience your absolute best!

"The common denominator for success is work."

John D. Rockefeller
(1839-1937)

Good things usually
do not happen to people
who do nothing.

Good things happen to people
who <u>make</u> things happen.

*"No act of kindness,
no matter how small,
is ever wasted."*

Aesop
(620-560 BC)

The smallest effort at serving others can provide great benefits to those you serve, and to yourself.

"If you aren't
going to go all the way,
why go at all?"

Joe Namath
Professional Football Hall of Famer

If you are not 100% committed
to the success of any idea,
project, or venture,
then why bother?

True happiness is not found in
half-measures, but in achieving
our greatest desires.

*"Be like a caterpillar:
enter your chrysalis,
prepare for the next phase
of your life,
and then
when it arrives—soar!"*

Dave Kelly

Everything up to the point you actually begin the pursuit of your passions is your "getting ready" phase, your chrysalis.

Then, when you break free, you are ready to fly and achieve beyond what you have ever done before.

*"In the confrontation between
the stream and the rock,
the stream always wins...*

*not through strength,
but through perseverance."*

H. Jackson Brown, Jr.
Author

Perseverance can move the unmovable force and lead to success.

Just like the stream.

It never quits.

Neither should you.

"Treat your time like your most valuable asset."

Dave Kelly

Wasting time is
like wasting money.

Once it's gone,
you can never get it back.

Spend it wisely.

*"I would rather have
a good plan today
than a perfect plan
two weeks from now."*

General George S. Patton
(1885-1945)

Do you have an idea, concept, or direction for something of value in your life?

Get started!

Too many people believe that everything has to be perfect before they can try to do anything so they do nothing and regret it for the rest of their lives.

I'll take action over "perfection" any day.

"If God is for me,
who can be against me?"

Romans 8:31

There is a great power in
understanding that God
is on your side.

He always is, even if you are
not aware of it at the moment.

*"If you can count
all your assets,
you always show
a profit."*

Robert Quillen
(1887-1948)

Consider your blessings
and feel blessed.

Your blessings are more
numerous than your challenges
and can be counted.

God wants you to have a
positive balance on your
ledger of life.

You are your own joy.

"One of your
greatest possessions
is the 24 hours
directly in front of you."

Anonymous

Consider time to be an asset,
an investment.

Seek the highest return
you can get by making the most
of all of your 24/7's.

*"More gold
has been mined
from the thoughts of men
than has ever been taken
from the earth."*

Napolean Hill
(1883-1970)

What is inside of you is more valuable than what the outside world sees.

You are your most valuable resource.

"Everything is possible!"

Dave Kelly

There is not a wish, goal, or
dream that comes into your
mind that you cannot achieve.

You must be willing to pay
the price and put forth the effort
necessary to realize it.

*"The best way
to make
your dreams come true
is to wake up."*

Paul Valery
(1871-1945)

When you start to pursue
your passions, it is like waking
up from a long sleep
during which you have beautiful
dreams.

You see things more clearly,
completely, and with a focus you
never thought possible.

This will allow you to turn
dreams into realities.

*"I'd rather be a failure
at something I enjoy
than to be a success
at something I hate."*

George Burns
(1896-1996)

Life is too short to spend it doing something you hate.

Find something you love and then find someone to pay you for doing it.

"I can do all things through Christ who strengthens me."

Philippians 4:13

Depend on your faith
to give you the power
to persevere and overcome
all obstacles in the way of
the realization of your dreams.

"Volunteers must be recognized.

Treat them like the most precious of treasures."

Dave Kelly

Reward the people
who go out of their way
to give of themselves.

They don't have to be there,
but because they are,
they will go as far as
you are willing to take them.

"A ship in harbor is safe—
but that is not
what ships are for."

John A. Shedd
Author

Take a chance.

Step outside your personal harbor (your limitations) and set sail on the high seas towards getting what you want out of life.

It may not be safe, but the pursuit of your passions will bring you immeasurable joy.

"God has given us two hands, one to receive with and the other to give with."

Billy Graham
Evangelist

God has given you some tremendous gifts and abilities.

Use them to give to others and you will receive great rewards.

"No one can make you
feel inferior
without your consent."

Eleanor Roosevelt
(1884-1962)

You choose whether you will be
a victim or down-trodden.

Do not give permission
to anyone to make you feel less
than the victor you can be.

*"Be a first rate version
of yourself,
not a second rate version
of someone else."*

Judy Garland
(1922-1969)

You are the best you
in the world.

Regardless of the setbacks
you endure, there is no one
in the world better at being you.

You have the opportunity
to be great, just like every other
person born into this world.

Pursue your greatness!

*"We are in
a big ol' fish tank
called life."*

Lydia Kathleen Kelly
3-year-old Philosopher

We are always being watched by
someone, no matter how
big or small.

The example we set can lift
others up or bring them down.

Be an example of all that
is positive in life and
show, through your actions,
how your spirit soars.

"I would like you to be free from concern."

1 Corinthians 7:32

God has called us to pursue
our mission in life, as He has
set it forth.

When we are doing what
He wants us to do,
then there is no need for worry.

We live in His Grace.

*"To change one's life:
start immediately.*

Do it flamboyantly.

No exceptions."

William James
(1842-1910)

Not happy with your life?

Change it.

Be bold!

Go for the "brass ring"!

Get out of your rut, and do it today.

Do not be bashful about aggressively pursuing your dreams.

"Ultimately your life and how you react to challenges may come down to one pivotal moment.

Seize that moment and create victory."

Dave Kelly

Keep your eyes open!

You never know when you will encounter a pivotal moment.

Be willing to seize opportunities and see them through to success.

*"Boldness does not
just happen—
you choose to be it."*

Denise Rowley
College Student

It takes boldness to achieve anything you want in life.

You can overcome enormous personal challenges, physical and financial limitations, and biases to succeed.

It's a matter of choosing to do so.

Be bold.

"Do not be afraid of adversity: acknowledge it, overcome it, conquer it."

Dave Kelly

Never allow adversity to become
a barrier for you.

You may lose "battles"
along the way, but if you think
like a victor, you will win
in the end.

"Delight yourself in the Lord and He will give you the desires of your heart."

Psalm 37:4

God wants you to be happy.

He wants you to find joy in your life, career, and family.

Pursue the passions of your heart and heavenly joy will follow.

"The people who get on in the world are the people who get up and look for circumstances they want, and if they can't find them, make them."

George Bernard Shaw
(1856-1950)

Be your own person and do not let the world decide who you are.

Don't just get by.

Make a way that allows you to flourish.

*"Reality can destroy
the dream;
why shouldn't the dream
destroy reality."*

George Moore
(1873-1958)

Every great idea, thought, or invention started as a dream, opposed to the reality of the time.

The light bulb, automobile, computer, and many other things we take for granted were once not part of reality.

Create the next "big thing" by destroying reality.

*"If you underestimate me, then
that is your perception…*

and my challenge."

Dave Kelly

If someone underestimates you,
don't give in to their perception.

Tell them to "bring it on"
and take it as a challenge to
overcome.

"The reason a lot of people do not recognize opportunity is because it usually goes around wearing overalls looking like hard work."

Thomas Edison
(1847-1931)

Work hard and persist and you will enjoy success while others never even get started.

*"He who touches the most
people will be remembered."*

Dave Kelly

Your greatest legacy is the service you perform and the lives you affect.

Create memories in granite.

"For even the Son of Man
came not to be served,
but to serve,
and offer His life
as a ransom for many."

Mark 10:45

We are called to serve others, even to the point of laying our life down to save someone else.

*"When one reaches out
to help another,
he touches the face of God."*

Walt Whitman
(1819-1892)

Service to others is the kind of thing that should become second nature to us.

"Failure is not forever."

Dave Kelly

Set-backs may happen along your journey to success.

Don't give in to them.

Find another path.

"Don't be afraid of
public speaking.

You are the expert
on your message.

Define it.

Shape it.

Share it."

Dave Kelly

You are the only person in the world who knows what is in your presentation.

Deliver it with confidence, passion, and authenticity and the audience will be with you.

"You become successful
by helping others
become successful."

John D. Rockefeller
(1839-1937)

Be a mentor.

An opportunity maker.

Lift others up higher than they thought they could go.

The momentum you create will carry you with them.

*"I love the 'popping' sound
I hear when I am
home canning.*

*To me,
it is the sound of success."*

Dia Stokes Kelly
Editor, Event Planning Specialist,
and Home Canner

Home canning projects "pop" the lid when they seal properly.

That means it is a successful project.

Figure out what success sounds like for you.

Seek that sound in everything you do.

*"Hitch your wagon
to a star."*

Ralph Waldo Emerson
(1803-1882)

Find someone who is successful at what you want to do.

Follow them, learn from them, and emulate them.

If you connect with a "star" in any endeavor you pursue, they will elevate you to heights you never thought possible.

"Effective planning leads to success."

Dave Kelly

Failure to plan leads to failure.

Resolve that you will plan every day to be successful.

*"How old would you be
if you didn't know
how you old you are?"*

Satchel Paige
(1906?-1982)

Live the age that you feel or think you are—you will never be "old."

*"We dream,
not so much because
we want to,
or because we like to,
but because we must do so
in order to achieve
success in life."*

Dave Kelly

Define your life by successes
that you choose, not by
remaining in mediocrity.

Determine your success by the
realization of your dreams.

"The Lord is my Shepherd,
I shall not want."

Psalm 23:1

You are protected by the Creator of the Universe who will always provide for you.

"Do the dreaded thing first."

Dave Kelly

That which you do not want to do must be the thing you begin your day with.

When you get the clutter out of your life and remove the dreaded things, then you will give your day energy and excitement.

"Each second is precious.

Treat them like gold."

Dave Kelly

There are 60 seconds in every minute, 3600 seconds in every hour, and 86,400 seconds in every day.

It took you five seconds to read that first sentence.

How do you use your time?

Is every second productive?

Are you moving closer to your goals?

Use every second to fulfill your mission on earth.

*"Objects in mirror are closer
than they appear."*

Warning on the passenger side-view mirror
on American vehicles

This is just an excuse for the mirror not working properly.

Don't make excuses—make successes.

"Don't find a fault.

Find a remedy."

Henry Ford
(1863-1947)

Who is responsible?

Who cares?

Who is going to overcome?

You are!

"Integrity is not negotiable."

Dave Kelly

If you always operate from an unwavering sense of integrity, then you will be able to chart the right path for your life.

*"Pay attention
to where you are going,
not where you are."*

Dia Stokes Kelly
Editor, Event Planning Specialist,
and Home Canner

Keep your sight on your final destination, not on the bumps and obstacles in the road.

That will keep you encouraged, rather than discouraged.

"Never aim for perfection.

Aim for success."

Anonymous

Don't wait for the perfect timing to initiate a project, start a new venture, or begin pursuing your passions.

Go and do—success will follow.

"Never fear 'No'."

Dave Kelly

Show the world how wonderful
you are.

Be the person you want to be.

Do not seek to impress others,
but impress them anyway with
your confidence, enthusiasm,
and focus.

"A man who carries a cat by the tail learns something that he can learn no other way."

Mark Twain
(1835-1910)

You may be surprised by what you will learn when you try something new.

You might find success, maybe pain, but you will definitely know something new.

*"Security is not
the absence of insecurity."*

Dave Kelly

Security comes from pursuing your dreams and making your own happiness, not cowering in a corner, afraid to take chances.

*"Commit your work
to the Lord,
then your plans will succeed."*

Proverbs 16:3

The best "business" partner
anyone can have is God.

Let Him control your plans and
He will perfect them for good.

*"Becoming
an overnight success
may take
your entire life."*

Dave Kelly

Be diligent in pursuing your dreams and you will achieve them, even if it takes the rest of your time on earth.

"There are enemies
of your efforts to succeed.

Sometimes they are called
family and friends."

Dave Kelly

Don't let those closest to you fill your head with negativity.

Think positively and make your own success.

"High achievement always take place in the framework of high expectation."

Charles F. Kettering
(1876-1958)

I expect to achieve great results in everything I try.

Do you?

Believe that you can achieve.

You will receive what you perceive.

"The greatest truth
in the universe
is that the power
to accomplish anything
is within you."

Dave Kelly

Most people use such a small part of their potential.

It doesn't have to be that way.

Tell yourself that limitations, barriers, and negativity have no place in your life.

You will be more than ordinary.

You will push yourself to go the extra little bit that is the difference between success and mediocrity.

*"You cannot
raise yourself up
by tearing
someone else down."*

Dave Kelly

You raise yourself up by lifting up others!

If all you have is negativity, put-downs, or criticisms of someone—lock them away in a vault.

Find a way to encourage and inspire other people and you will find incredible strength for yourself.

*"What we have done
for ourselves alone
dies with us;
what we have done
for others and the world
remains and is immortal."*

Albert Pike
(1809-1891)

If we have no impact on the world, then we will only live on in the memories of those who knew us.

If we impact the world, then we will live on in the memory of many who never met us.

"Never confuse a single defeat with a final defeat."

F. Scott Fitzgerald
(1896-1940)

Don't let setbacks and challenges lead you to complete defeat.

Instead, use defeats as challenges to overcome and as stepping stones to victory.

"I have the ability and talent from God to make my dreams come true."

Dave Kelly

This belief is what motivates me on a daily basis.

I have no doubt that I will be successful in everything I pursue, with the hand of God guiding me.

"Dream dreams,
pursue passions,
and find that which makes
your life worthwhile."

Dave Kelly

Spend your life and career doing things you enjoy and you will be able to look back on a life fulfilled.

About The Author

Dave Kelly is a professional speaker, trainer, author, and humorist and publishes a monthly e-newsletter, *Gonzo Motivation*. He travels the United States extensively, speaking for high school, college and university students, corporations, churches, and at conferences and conventions. With his wife's assistance, he is the creator of a number of leadership programs on topics such as – but not limited to – personal and group motivation, team building, conflict resolution, communication, time management, goal attainment, confidence in leadership, study skills, public speaking, event planning and fundraising.

A native of Wisconsin, Dave is an avid Green Bay Packers fan. He has been involved with the Kiwanis Family for more than 25 years and enjoys volunteering at a local elementary school, reading stories to Kindergarteners and first graders. He hopes one day to publish his own original story for children of all ages, *George, The Drobble*.

Dave lives in Atlanta with his wife, daughter and numerous cats. He also has another daughter in college.

For more information on Dave, his programs, and/or to subscribe to his e-newsletter, please visit his web site at www.gonzospeaks.com or call his office at (770) 552-6592.

Printed in the United States
65000LVS00001B/67-90

9 781425 957674